Tools We Use
Chefs

Instrumentos de trabajo
Los chefs

Dana Meachen Rau

Marshall Cavendish
Benchmark
New York

The kitchen is busy!

A chef is getting dinner ready.

---❖---

¡En la cocina hay mucho trabajo!

Un chef está preparando la comida.

The *menu* lists many foods.

It shows what the chef can make for dinner.

El *menú* es una lista de muchos platos de comida.

Muestra lo que el chef puede preparar para la cena.

A chef wears a white jacket.

He wears a tall white hat.

———❖———

Un chef se pone una chaqueta blanca.

Se pone un gorro alto y blanco.

A chef starts each day at the market.

She needs to buy fresh foods.

———————◆———————

Una chef empieza cada día en el mercado.

Necesita comprar alimentos frescos.

She buys lots of vegetables.

She buys fish and meat.

---❖---

Ella compra muchas verduras.

Compra pescado y carne.

In his kitchen, a chef cuts on a cutting board.

His knives come in many sizes.

❖

En la cocina, un chef corta sobre una tabla de cortar.

Sus cuchillos son de muchos tamaños.

He fills a *measuring cup*.

The cup helps him use just the right amount.

❖

Él llena una *taza para medir*.

La taza lo ayuda a usar la cantidad exacta.

He puts his *ingredients* in a pot.

He adds salt and pepper.

❖

Él pone los *ingredientes* en una olla.

Agrega sal y pimienta.

The stove heats up the pot.

He stirs the pot with a spoon.

❖

La olla se calienta en la estufa.

Él revuelve la comida en la olla con una cuchara.

He puts the meat in a pan.

He cooks it in the oven.

————❖————

Él pone la carne en una sartén.

La cocina en el horno.

The stove and oven get hot.

The chef protects his hands with a thick cloth.

---❖---

La estufa y el horno se calientan.

El chef se protege las manos con una tela gruesa.

He cleans up spills.

He is always careful in the kitchen.

———————❖———————

Él limpia lo que se derrama.

Siempre es cuidadoso en la cocina.

The food is ready to serve.

The chef has used her tools to make a meal.

———————❖———————

La comida está lista para servir.

La chef ha usado sus instrumentos para preparar platos de comida.

Tools Chefs Use
Instrumentos de trabajo de los chefs

cutting board
tabla de cortar

fresh food
alimentos frescos

measuring cup
taza para medir

menu
menú

28

pan
sartén

pot
olla

stove
estufa

Challenge Words

ingredients The foods a chef needs to make a meal.

measuring cup A cup with marks on the side to show how much.

menu The list of foods a chef can make.

Vocabulario avanzado

ingredientes Los alimentos que un chef necesita para preparar una comida.

taza para medir Una taza con marcas en los lados para medir las cantidades.

menú La lista de platos de comida que un chef sabe preparar.

29

Index

Page numbers in **boldface** are illustrations.

chef, 2, **3**, 4, 6, **7**, 8, 12, **13**, 22, 26
cooking, 20
cutting board, 12, **13**, **28**

dinner, 2, 4

fish, 10, **11**
food, 4, 26
fresh food, 8, **9**, **11**, **28**

ingredients, 16, 29

kitchen, 2, **3**, 24
knives, 12, **13**

market, 8, **9**
meal, 26
measuring cup, 14, **15**, **28**, 29
meat, 10, **11**, 20, **21**
menu, 4, **5**, **28**, 29

oven, 20, 22

pan, 20, **21**, **29**
pepper, 16
pot, 16, **17**, 18, **19**, **29**
protection, 22

salt, 16
serve, 26
spills, 24
spoon, 18, **19**
stove, 18, **19**, 22, **23**, **29**

vegetables, 10, **11**

white hat, 6, **7**
white jacket, 6, **7**

Índice

Los números en **negrita** corresponden a páginas con ilustraciones.

alimentos frescos, 8, **9**, **11**, **28**

carne, 10, **11**, 20, **21**
chaqueta blanca, 6, **7**
chef, 2, **3**, 4, 6, **7**, 8, 12, **13**, 22, 26
(él) cocina, 20
(la) cocina, 2, **3**, 24
comida, 2, 4, 26, **27**
cuchara, 18, **19**
cuchillos, 12, **13**

estufa, 18, **19**, 22, **23**, **29**

gorro blanco, 6, **7**

horno, 20, 22

ingredientes, 16, 29

menú, 4, **5**, **28**, 29
mercado, 8, **9**

olla, 16, **17**, 18, **19**, **29**

pescado, 10, **11**
pimienta, 16
platos de comida, 4, 26
protección, 22

sal, 16
sartén, 20, **21**, **29**
se derrama, 24
servir, 26

tabla de cortar, 12, **13**, **28**
taza para medir, 14, **15**, **28**, 29

verduras, 10, **11**

About the Author

Dana Meachen Rau is an author, editor, and illustrator. A graduate of Trinity College in Hartford, Connecticut, she has written more than one hundred fifty books for children, including nonfiction, biographies, early readers, and historical fiction. She lives with her family in Burlington, Connecticut.

With thanks to the Reading Consultants:

Nanci Vargus, Ed.D., is an Assistant Professor of Elementary Education at the University of Indianapolis.

Beth Walker Gambro received her M.S. Ed. Reading from the University of St. Francis, Joliet, Illinois.

Sobre la autora

Dana Meachen Rau es escritora, editora e ilustradora. Graduada del Trinity College de Hartford, Connecticut, ha escrito más de ciento cincuenta libros para niños, entre ellos libros de ficción histórica y de no ficción, biografías y libros de lectura para principiantes. Vive con su familia en Burlington, Connecticut.

Con agradecimiento a las asesoras de lectura:

Nanci R. Vargus, Dra. en Ed., es profesora ayudante de educación primaria en la Universidad de Indianápolis.

Beth Walker Gambro recibió su Maestría en Ciencias de la Educación, con especialización en Lectura, de la Universidad de St. Francis, en Joliet, Illinois.

Marshall Cavendish Benchmark
99 White Plains Road
Tarrytown, New York 10591-9001
www.marshallcavendish.us

Text copyright © 2008 by Marshall Cavendish Corporation

Library of Congress Cataloging-in-Publication Data

Rau, Dana Meachen, 1971–
[Chefs. English & Spanish]
Los chefs / by Dana Meachen Rau = Chefs / de Dana Meachen Rau.
p. cm. – (Bookworms. Tools we use = losInstrumentos de trabajo)
Includes index.
Text in English and Spanish.
ISBN-13: 978-0-7614-2822-0 (bilingual edition) – ISBN-13: 978-0-7614-2798-8 (spanish edition)
ISBN-13: 978-0-7614-2657-8 (english edition)
1. Kitchen utensils–Juvenile literature. 2. Cookery–Juvenile literature.
I. Title. II. Title: Los chefs
TX656.R3812 2008
643'.3–dc22
2007013914

Spanish Translation and Text Composition by
Victory Productions, Inc.

Photo Research by Anne Burns Images

Cover Photo by *Jupiter Images*/Comstock Images

The photographs in this book are used with permission and through the courtesy of:
Jupiter Images: pp. 1, 15, 28BL FoodPix/Wendell Webber; pp. 5, 28BR Comstock Images;
pp. 11, 28TR FoodPix; pp. 23, 29R FoodPix/Scott Payne; p. 25 Blend Images/Andersen Ross.
SuperStock: pp. 3, 19 age fotostock. *Woodfin Camp*: p. 7 Chuck Fishman;
pp. 13, 28TL Catherine Karnow. *Corbis*: p. 9 Pelletier Micheline/Sygma;
pp. 17, 29C Turbo/zefa; pp. 21, 20, 29L photocuisine/ P. Desgrieux; p. 27 Dave Bartruff.

Printed in Malaysia
1   3   5   6   4   2